REFLECTIONS

in the Life of a Poet

Reflections in the Life of a Poet
by Don and Anne Dilley
Copyright © 2009 Tangled Web Press

Edited by:
Elaine S. Polin
Richard Brotbeck

Cover Art by:
Jane Hickok Reid

Cover Layout by:
Richard Brotbeck

All Rights Reserved.

Reflections in the Life of a Poet
by Don and Anne Dilley
Copyright © 2009 Tangled Web Press

ISBN 978-0-9825876-0-7

Tangled Web Press
PO Box 233
Shawnee Mission, KS 66201

http://blog.poetsofmars.com

REFLECTIONS
in the Life of a Poet

A NOTE FROM THE AUTHOR

The cover art is a painting by Jane Hickok Reid. She was a descendant of the infamous James Butler (Wild Bill) Hickok. She painted this shortly before losing her sight due to complications of diabetic retinopathy. Jane died in October, 1998. The painting has been donated for our use by her daughter, Anne Reid Dilley, my lovely co-author and wife.

FOREWORD

Sometimes I sit up late at night and ponder our follies and fates. In the past, when I thought about poetry, I couldn't help but wonder what happened. Where did Eugene Field and Emily Dickinson go?

Today, I believe I've stumbled across part of the answer. Poetry has faded from grace because it has been hijacked by critics and intellectuals.

This is not a modern perception. Good poets have been prefacing their works with jabs at the snobbery for two hundred years.

Many collections of poetry begin by quoting something like, "Studying literature at Harvard is like learning about women at the Mayo Clinic." (Roy Blount, Jr.).

I hope this book qualifies as one of those.

If it does, it will because the readers were able to connect with Don Dilley, not because the reviewers and critics were unable to.

Don and I have deep Southern roots. We are unashamed of our simple upbringings and slow-paced ways. We lay on the countrified charm thick and we still tip our hats to gentlemen and open doors for ladies.

As you read his words, you will see that Don is more of a lyricist. Each of these pieces needs a guitar and fiddle accompaniment. Please, gather round with your Mom and them and read these aloud.

Richard Brotbeck

INTRODUCTION

I sit here with pen in hand, to write poetry that tells a story. I am not a writer trying to correct the ills of the world, but I write stories of everyday life and people. I write nonsensical verse for the fun of rhythm and rhyme.

I have written these pages to entertain, and maybe enlighten those who read my words. Most of my work is done in metered rhyme. That is what I learned by reading early in life, and still prefer to do.

I learned to read using "A CHILD'S GARDEN OF VERSES," by Robert Louis Stevenson. Although the original book was destroyed in a flood in 1973, I have obtained a slightly later edition that I still read on occasion.

I have maintained an ongoing affair with rhyming poetry my entire life, and have learned to appreciate and like unrhymed poetry. I wrote my first rhyme at the age of ten for my fourth grade teacher who had been out sick for a few days. I became "teacher's pet" for the remainder of the year, and found it to be not an unpleasant experience.

Since that first poem, I have found that rhyming verse would come to me at many varied times and circumstances. I might see something while driving that sparks a thought, and from that will come a poem.

I have many times in my daily routine as an industrial electrician and programmer, found that a particular occurrence would trigger a poem about subjects ranging from serious to frivolous.

As a young adult, I was fortunate enough to play in a couple of amateur rock and roll bands. This gave me a feeling for the meters of poetic expression. I see songs as poetry with musical accompaniment. Now at age 63, I do not have any less love for poetry or music, and write my poems in a manner in which they may easily be set to music.

I have been fortunate enough to become acquainted with a group known as "The Poets of Mars." They meet on the Internet to discuss poetry and explore new as well as ancient forms of poetry. This experience has enriched my life, and the lives of others from around the world.

I have asked my wife Anne to share in this pleasure with me, as we have shared so many wonderful things in the past.

I hope your time spent reading this book will give you the enjoyment I have had in the writing of it.

Don Dilley

DEDICATION

It would take another book to list everyone to whom I would like to dedicate this book.

That being said, I dedicate this book in memory of my father, Don C. Dilley, Sr., for giving me his love of rhythm and rhyme and to my loving and supportive wife Anne. Without her indulgence, this project might never have gotten started.

I would also like to dedicate this book to all the "Poets of Mars," who have been instrumental in critiquing, praising, and inspiring many of these works. Last but not least, my Editor and friend, Elaine S. Polin and my Publisher and friend, Richard (T.D. Euwaite) Brotbeck.

REFLECTIONS

in the Life of a Poet

Chapter One

SINGING

Sometimes we sing a happy song,
Sometimes we sing so sad.
A song can make us feel the love,
That we all wish we had.

Some days we say we have the Blues,
But Blues is just a song,
On days when you're not flying high,
Then sing the Bluesy songs.

So try some Do-Wop or some Jazz,
Or maybe Rock and Roll.
Somewhere you'll find the perfect sound,
To lift your troubled soul.

So sing to me and sing to us,
Or sing it to yourself.
The worst thing you can do to song,
Is leave it on the shelf.

A DIFFERENT MANSION

When does a house become a home,
Must it be small or large?
A mansion on the highest hill,
One room upon a barge?

My home is where my heart resides,
It does not matter where.
A mansion of the greatest kind,
With love for all who's there.

So visit in my mansion home,
The one I keep inside.
And share your love with those of us,
Who in this house abide.

My mansion is a loving home,
It welcomes all to stay.
And gives a hand to those in need,
To help them on their way.

SEA IN LOVE

Upon the sand you stand and look,
Your face is all aglow,
The moon reflecting in your eyes
Lights up all here below.

I wish to touch your lovely legs,
And hold you by your waist,
I long to wrap around your form,
Your silky skin to taste.

I'll hold you up atop a wave,
Caress you as you swim,
For I am strong and full of life,
And you are soft and thin.

Can you, my love, feel now my words,
While wrapped in my embrace?
Now does the feel of me on you,
Cause your warm heart to race?

Oh, yes, my love, I am the sea,
I am in love with you,
Of all the ladies in this world
You are the one who's true.

PAINTING IN THE ATTIC

A painting found of beauty fair,
Up in the attic high,
A lovely lady all in white,
Is flanked by light blue sky.

A dusty canvas hidden there,
Found quite by accident,
The frame was gilded with thin gold,
And nowhere was it rent.

This lovely girl with smile so bright,
And lovely eyes of blue,
Created longing in my heart,
To know more than I do.

I asked my mother who she was,
My mother did not know,
But then my grandma said she knew,
Her mother told her so.

A painting done of great grandma,
In wedding dress of white,
The hoop skirt flowing all about,
Made quite a gorgeous sight.

The eyes of blue so full of fire,
They sparkled like a star,
And not a blemish on the face,
Her visage to then mar.

The painting hung above the fire,
Down in the grand ballroom,
'Twas placed there on her wedding day
By her new loving groom.

Until the day she lost her sight,
In honor there it hung,
Her blue eyes got as dark as coal,
The memory then stung.

So to the attic then consigned,
For many lonely years,
The thought of it gave her much grief,
And caused her many tears.

Now she is gone and grandma too,
And mother's gone away,
The painting's on my mantel piece,
And that's where it will stay.

My great grandma was quite a girl,
Great granddad loved her so,
I hope to meet her once again,
When it's my turn to go.

BEE'S KNEES

While sitting in my easy chair,
I closed my weary eyes,
I heard a buzzing in my ears,
Much as a bunch of flies.

I looked around inside my mind,
To find this noisy buzz,
And what I found put me in shock,
It looked like navel fuzz.

But then upon a close exam,
With jeweler's loupe I see,
A tiny field there in the lens
Where only fuzz should be.

The colors there of red and green,
Of yellow and of blue,
I see the flowers and the grass
In every single hue.

The buzzing now is louder still,
Much closer I approach,
I do not know who owns this field,
Not sure I should encroach.

But yes, I see then what it is,
Ten thousand tiny bees,
They're drinking nectar from the blooms
While kneeling on their knees.

So now the buzzing has been found,
And now I can be calm,
I think I'll drift now, off to sleep,
The buzz a soothing balm.

NEW BEGINNING

Awake, awake, arise, arise,
Open my mind, open my eyes,
It's way past dawn, there's much to say,
Who will I choose to be this day?

A sailing master, brave and true,
Sailing the horn with expert crew?
A fighter pilot in the sky?
A baker making apple pie?

You see I can be who I please,
For with my pen I tell and tease,
I'll make up something new to say,
And show it to the world today.

For now I think I'll just be me,
A poet is what I will be,
I'll write a rhyme just for the fun,
I'll kiss the girls to watch them run.

Some run out and some run in,
Either way it makes me grin,
Tomorrow, who knows what I'll be,
I guess we'll wait till then to see.

RUDY REDDINGTON

My name is Rudy Reddington,
Of you I am a part,
I travel through your arteries,
Pumped by your beating heart.

Into the lungs my journey goes,
For there I turn bright red,
And then I take the nourishment,
Up to your thinking head.

I also travel to the feet,
And to the finger tips,
Your skin is also on my route,
As well as both your lips.

You see I go most everywhere,
I give your body life,
So when you carve the ham tonight,
Be careful with that knife.

I flow along my carefree way,
I change from red to blue,
And then I start the trip again,
To give sweet life to you.

BREATH OF LIFE

Sometimes when eyes are closed in sleep,
My breath will pause a bit,
Or else I snore so very loud
My ribs, my wife will hit.

A test I took, a mask I wore,
But I could not breathe well,
The tech came in and checked it out,
Was bad and she could tell.

She stood me up and heimliched me,
And out came a surprise,
Three ballads and a couplet rhyme,
And sonnet did arise.

The night went by from that time on,
No problems did they see,
It seems the troubles all were caused,
By breathing poetry.

SHIPWRECKED

A shipwreck when I was a lad,
A fiery crash indeed,
So many died a gruesome death,
So many were in need.

We're stranded here in no-man's land,
Up on a mountain high,
We're stuck forever here on Earth,
An island in the sky.

I long for home, my lovely place,
The place to lay my head,
What a joy to just once more,
Lay down upon my bed.

The ship is strong, it is rebuilt,
But it won't leave this dale,
For though the ship has been renewed,
We have no solar sail.

Someday we'll build our sail so strong,
And take off toward the stars,
The first stop will be home of course,
Up there on planet Mars.

REFLECTIONS
by Anne Dilley

You and me
Dressed all in white
In a large room
Bathed in light,
Doors open to the night air,
Curtains billowing in the breeze.

An unseen hand
Directs an unseen orchestra,
We come together,
Slowly we begin to dance,
Sometimes slow, sometimes faster
Moving in and out of the doors.

There is no one but the two of us
Dancing, dreaming, twirling,
Shy, bold,
Playful, dramatic,
Laughing, loving,
Passionate.

One man,
One woman,
Two people
In awe
In love
Forever.

Like a shared dream,
We see images all around us
Of who we were,
Who we are and
Who we will be?
Reflections.

CARMELITA

Black velvet in a gilded frame,
Hung here upon my wall,
Your likeness looks at me each day,
I made sure you can't fall.

Your festive dress, red, green and blue,
Sails up as round you twirl,
I am in love with what I see,
A lovely dancing girl.

Your midnight eyes and matching hair,
Your smile of crimson too,
These work together in my mind,
I fall in love with you.

The softness of your velvet skin,
The curves beneath your dress,
I stare at you each lonely day,
To relieve all my stress.

I saw you on the street that day,
My heart jumped to my throat,
I had to bring you home with me,
Now I this rhyme emote.

Now Carmelita hanging there,
A picture that is fine,
This entire planet have I searched,
And now you're truly mine.

THE HAPPY MAN

Today I met a happy man,
He was a lot like me,
A lot of trouble he has seen,
And more he still may see.

A smile upon his weathered face,
A sparkle in his eye,
A voice that went within my head,
He uttered not a sigh.

He said his happiness was true,
It could not be called fake,
He had the love of lady Anne,
He still lived for her sake.

He met her when he was so down,
No smile upon his face,
She taught him how to love again,
And how to run this race.

He writes his rhymes for all to read,
He hopes they all enjoy,
They sometimes take his work with them,
Like it's a tinker toy.

I meet this man near every day,
He's always in this place,
I meet him when I comb my hair,
And when I shave my face.

MOONLIGHT RENDEZVOUS

Your silken skin is all aglow,
Bathed in the moon's soft light,
Your body, nude from head to toe,
Is really quite a sight.

We run across the sandy beach,
Into the rippling tide,
Secluded beach for us alone,
No reason we should hide.

To swim and play out in the surf,
A pleasure in this life,
This love we have grows stronger still,
For we are man and wife.

Hold me in your arms so soft,
I'll hold you tight in mine,
We'll share a laugh and then a sip,
Of homemade apple wine.

The taste of love will fill the air,
I'll take you by your wrist,
And hand in hand we'll make our way,
Back through the salty mist.

SILENCE IS LONELY

My mountain home is silent now,
My love has gone away,
She rests beneath yon old oak tree,
The place she picked to stay.

The orange globe that's climbing high,
Has lost much of its light,
The warmth has gone from its bright glow,
It's now as cool as night.

The emerald trees have lost their sheen,
The birds sing bitter songs,
When she was here the bluebells rang,
As if they were brass gongs.

The forest sounds are silent now,
The creatures miss her sight,
She loved them all, they loved her too,
And all the world seemed bright.

I hope someday the bluebird's song
Is heard here in this glen,
As we two hand in hand will stroll
When I, too meet my end.

REFLECTIONS

in the Life of a Poet

Chapter Two

MEMORIAL DAY

Our bones lie here, in cold hard ground,
Alone but in a crowd.
Some of us in clothes interred,
And some in but a shroud.

We fought in wars and there we died,
We all thought we were right.
And now in sleep the dead do weep,
Throughout this endless night.

Each year we see the ones who bring,
The flowers to us here.
And though we have no hearts to feel,
It fills our bones with cheer.

Remembered souls can come to life,
As fleeting memories.
Yes, even those who sank in ships,
Out on embattled seas.

This day each year is set aside,
So you remember us.
We like to see you bringing gifts,
And making such a fuss.

Then back to sleep this lonely sleep,
This sleep that never ends.
Except that special day each year,
When honored by our friends.

REAL MEN DO CRY

I lay in wait my gun in hand,
I do this in a foreign land.
A war is why I am right here,
I am a man, I have no fear.

It matters not why I need fight,
From early morn till dead of night.
I see the man that I must kill,
An easy shot atop this hill.

I aim my rifle, see his face,
I know that death he'll soon embrace.
I think of words I learned in youth,
And pray that they had been the truth.

A tear from eyes that are intent,
On seeing where the bullet's sent.
Tells me I wish it was not so,
But in a blink his life will go.

My tears for him I'm told are wrong,
That I should dance and sing a song.
They say a real man never cries,
How can he not, when someone dies.

WORD PAINTING

I have a picture in my head,
No canvas, paint, or brush.
This picture I must now create,
As words from my mind rush.

The light blue sky starts at the top,
Blue ocean down below.
The white caps splashing to the sky,
Shows how the winds now blow.

Way off we see white sails of ships,
Up close the seagulls fly.
The red and blue and white of flags,
Are flying through the sky.

Off to my right a beach of tan,
Beside a dark gray clift.
The bright green grass upon the top,
Above the reddish rift.

These thing I see here in my mind,
I show them now to you.
I hope you see what I now paint,
With words I feel are true.

TRIBUTE TO THE TEACHERS

There is a very special group,
Who go forth every day.
To face another special group,
And show to them the way.
That way is knowledge, truth and light,
That way is what they teach.
They try to tell our precious kids,
And show them goals to reach.
They sometimes put their very life,
Upon the chopping block.
But through it all they still stand fast,
Stand fast as if a rock.
Each child they teach is one more seed,
To sprout and then unfurl.
Those kids they teach now will soon be,
The leaders of this world.
Our teachers will instill the best,
In all our children's minds.
To make them adults, smart and proud,
They won't be left behind.
So let me say to all who read,
These words I put down here.
Give praise to all our teachers now,
And raise a hearty cheer.
For my own self, I'll tell them now,
I do appreciate.
The work you do so well I see,
Will gain you heaven's gate.
You teach our young and watch them grow,
You teach them right from wrong.
To thank you for this selfless work,
I'll write this little song.
It is the way I have this day,
To say, "thanks for my son."
To tell you now, I thank you all,
It is a job well done.

RESPECT

Much has been said and also wrote,
About the word respect.
What does it take to give and get,
Should we just genuflect.

Respect's a thing we want to get,
A thing we need to give.
What is the cost of this small word,
To have it where we live.

It can't be bought at any price,
It must be rightly earned.
It can't be sold for cash or gold,
The money's better burned.

It must be given free of will,
No charge or any strings.
To get respect, you must first give,
The same with many things.

For he who cannot give his love,
Will die a lonely man.
And if respect he cannot give,
He'll end where he began.

For he who cannot give his love,
Will pay a heavy toll.
And if respect he cannot give,
Shall die a lonely soul.

GROWN UP
by Anne Dilley

I sit
And look at you
As you stare unseeingly at me—
Hour after hour.

Why can't we do more than just stare?

How I long
To run to you
To hold you
To love you.

To tell you
Everything that bottles up inside,
And frustrates me,
And makes me want to scream!

But I can't...Why not?

So long ago
You held the key
To all my dreams.
And now you just sit there—
A mockery of my old self
The old me
The child
That always wanted to be grown up.

I used to tell you everything
And I want to do it again.
But it's impossible now...
Big girls can't have teddy bears.

BATTLES

The dusty road was long and hot,
While walking home that day.
Another boy was walking too,
He stepped right in my way.

"What's in the bag?" he said to me,
"It's just some penny candy."
He wanted me to give it up,
He thought that would be dandy.

Five pieces in the bag I had,
For I had spent five cents.
He said tomorrow bring some more,
And make sure there were mints.

When I got to my Grandpa's house,
And asked what he'd have done.
I asked if I should stop to fight,
For he was only one.

And then the words he said to me,
Have lived with me since then.
Don't fight the battle on his terms,
For you will never win.

Next day I went again to buy,
Some candy in a sack,
And sure enough I met the boy,
As I was headed back.

I handed him the paper bag,
And went along my way.
I smiled at what my Grandpa did,
That dusty July day.

I pulled a bag from pocket deep,
And sucked a peppermint,
I wondered how the boy would do,
While chewing Feenamint.

The chocolate candy in the bag,
A big box of Ex-Lax.
I'll bet he'd rather run a race,
Barefoot on carpet tacks.

A lesson was to be learned here,
A lesson about terms,
I think I'll do some fishing now,
I must go dig some worms.

BALLAD OF THE TEN GAUGE

My Grandpa had a ten gauge gun,
It was as tall as me.
I begged and pleaded for one shot,
He would not hear my plea.

I wanted so to shoot that gun,
But he kept saying no.
He said it was too much for me,
So wait until I grow.

He got the gun from his grandpa,
Was what he said to me.
He pulled out one gigantic shell,
I got a good look-see.

For three long summers I did beg,
All three he still said no.
Finally he said I was grown,
Enough to have a go.

We walked outside, he placed a can,
Upon the barnyard fence.
I aimed the gun and shot it once,
And haven't shot it since.

My back was flat against the ground,
The pain an awesome fee.
The gun had knocked me to the ground,
And then thrown rocks at me.

That gun now hangs above the hearth,
A Civil War antique.
I save it for the day I get,
A really bad critique.

I will not shoot the critic, no.
Just let him shoot the gun.
To see the pain in his harsh smile,
To me should be much fun.

SEA OF LIFE

Two lovers sit upon the shore,
Of this vast sea of life,
As they sit hand in hand and look,
They contemplate their strife.

No matter if the times get hard,
Their love will see them through,
It bonds them close and warms their hearts
And turns their gray skies blue.

The daily trials of this life,
Will try to tear their love,
But it is held firm and intact
By faith in Him above.

A bond between two earthly souls,
No man may tear apart,
For each of them will hold a space
Within the other's heart.

The men will come and try to take
This woman from his grasp,
She's flattered but before she goes,
His firm hand she will clasp.

She'll feel his love all warm and soft,
She'll tell the stranger, "No,"
She'll wrap her love around her man,
She'll stay and not let go.

The same will happen to her mate,
When temptress comes his way,
He'll shut his eyes and see the face
Of her who makes him stay.

Two lovers sit upon the shore,
Of this vast sea of life,
And marvel at the joy they feel
Because they're man and wife.

Then each will say a little prayer,
To thank God for each other
And ask for help from Him above
For her to be a mother.

The pain and tears of giving birth,
Give way to happy joy,
The child they have has lots of love,
No matter, girl or boy.

As to an adult, this child grows,
They'll teach it right from wrong,
And every time the child is good
Their hearts will sing a song.

Until at last their child is grown,
And picks a lifelong mate,
And starts a family of its own,
It is predestined fate.

Two lovers sit upon the shore,
Two lovers, man and wife,
And marvel how they made it through,
This great vast sea of life.

NATURE'S SONG

Magnolias blooming in the spring,
Is such a sight to see,
While sitting on the sunny porch,
And sipping on my tea.

The bluebirds singing in the trees,
The lilacs all in bloom,
The perfect day to be a bride,
For just the perfect groom.

The roses with their fragrant blooms,
Grow in the flower beds,
The yellow of the daffodils
Will compliment the reds.

The robins hop along the ground,
The squirrels run up the tree,
The eagle soars high in the sky,
As they watch down at me.

The deer are grazing with the cows,
They have no need to fear,
There are no hunters with their guns,
They're safe while they are here.

So sit with me and while the time,
Sit here and drink some tea,
And watch with me as nature sings
Her song to you and me.

MOONBEAM DREAM

The moon is large and watches me.
As I look back at him,
For hours long we both have stared,
With faces set quite grim.

The first to blink will surely lose,
This battle of the eyes,
The face I see is just the same,
While it, through night sky, flies.

He moves so slowly, westward bound,
He dares me now to blink,
Wait, what was that I saw from him?
I saw him smile and wink.

Did I now win, or did I not,
A question that's quite deep,
For while I watched him in the sky,
I think I went to sleep.

HAZARDS OF WRITING

When I was young and in my prime,
I'd write a verse and make it rhyme,
I showed one to my teacher, wise,
She hated it, to my surprise.

She told me I could not write rhyme,
The way I wrote must be a crime,
She also said I'd write no prose,
It was as plain as my big nose.

I told her then to kiss my hiney,
And not to be so dadblamed whiney,
I thought that I could make her swoon,
I dropped my pants and flashed my moon.

My next stop was the office cold,
I walked right in, I was so bold,
The leader had an awful fit,
It was two days 'fore I could sit.

I wondered what she'd have to say,
If she could see me here today,
I packed my copy of my book,
And sent so she could have a look.

I got a note back in the mail,
Her mem'ry had begun to fail,
But though she looked and tried to see,
She said she couldn't remember me.

I sent one back, picture inside,
A snapshot of my big backside,
I wondered if she'd take a look,
She did and sent me back my book.

You still can't write and never will.
I said it once, I say it still,
I see you still have got the mark,
Where headman's paddle once did bark.

THE CHURCHYARD

The old churchyard up on the hill,
With headstones gray and white.
Is such a pretty sight to see,
As long as it's daylight.

But when the darkness hits the ground,
And light has gone away.
Those headstones seem to move around,
Until the morning grey.

On one such night there was no moon,
I looked up from my bed.
A figure moved atop the hill,
My heart was filled with dread.

The haze upon my window pane,
Made such an eerie glow.
Around the head of what I saw.
I wished it was not so.

To see this shape and still not know,
Just what it was I saw.
Made my mind want a closer look,
My being filled with awe.

Up from my bed and out the door,
I crept without a sound.
I heard the beat of my own heart,
As I crawled on the ground.

I made my way on hands and knees,
Up to the highest crest.
And what I saw on reaching there,
Gave me no chance to rest.

A group of ghouls and goblins too,
Were huddled in a ring.
With voices hushed so none could hear,
Their chanting they did sing.

Then from quite near, a voice so strong,
It pummeled me with fear.
I fathomed not the words it spoke,
But it was very clear.

The group got up and started off,
Down toward our sleepy town.
I ran back home and dialed the phone,
My face a massive frown.

I asked for sheriff Buford Tee,
Emergency I said.
They said, the sheriff's off tonight,
Just go on back to bed.

The sheriff's with a group of kids,
The graveyard is the site.
Rehearsing for "All Hallows Play,"
At school tomorrow night.

REFLECTIONS

in the Life of a Poet

Chapter Three

ANGEL ON THE STREET

As I walked down the street today,
A young girl sat alone,
Her back contained a nasty hump,
She let out a low moan.

The passers-by ignored the girl,
As if they could not see,
I walked on by just like the rest,
She turned and looked at me.

Forlorn she looked so sad and low,
I thought my heart would break,
I did not want to get involved,
I thought it a mistake.

Then turn I did and walked right back,
I asked her come with me,
I took her to the coffee shop,
To have some lunch with me.

And as we ate she looked at me,
Her sadness became smile,
I asked how long she sat out there,
"For just a little while."

So many people passed her,
And gave it nary thought,
She did not seem to mind at all,
A lesson I was taught.

She waited there for me to come,
And care for her this way,
The others could not see her there,
That is the angel's way.

She took the blanket from her back,
She tugged at my heart strings,
There on her back it was no hump,
But perfect angel's wings.

She told me that she's here for me,
To guard me through my life,
She'll help with matters great and small
That cause me pain and strife.

So if you see your angel there,
She might be all in rags,
Remember you're the one she wants,
And angels wear no tags.

SEDUCTRESS

The ocean here in front of me,
Goes on without an end,
Seducing men to come with her,
Their will she soon shall bend.

Aboard a sailing ship so strong,
A mighty man shall tread,
But should he break this mistress' heart,
He'll surely end up dead.

She'll throw a fit her waves will crash,
A mighty storm ensue,
She'll get revenge on one who cheats,
As well as me and you.

So heed me well, ye sailing crew,
Be true unto the sea,
And she will keep you safe and well,
And you'll be truly free.

Yes, sail across her waves and be
The love she will require,
You will then find you have become
Her heart's one great desire.

NATURE'S CHILD

Another day and all is well,
The glowing ball arises,
The grass is as an emerald,
With glistening surprises.

The morning haze a butterfly,
Ascending to the heights,
To leave behind the morning dew,
Like little sparkling lights.

The robin singing on the breeze,
The blue jay's rasping calls,
Like music to my listening ears,
Vibrating off the walls.

The sounds of nature all join in,
A mighty audio wave,
I feel a sense of being small,
A feeling hard to stave.

But through it all I've come to know,
That Nature's child am I,
The adventure never finds an end.
Until I say goodbye.

MOUNTAIN TOP MORNING

Alone here on this mountain top,
I sometimes hear the bunny hop,
The bluebirds sing their lovely tunes,
Some days I read these ancient runes.

The wind will whisper through the trees,
Before the hawk the rabbit flees,
The statues in the clouds on high,
All wink at me as they float by.

The morning, cool with mountain air.
I sit and watch without a care,
The dew has settled on the ground,
The bees are flying all around.

The hummingbirds from flowers eat,
I see these things here from my seat,
One lady orchestrates it all,
For Mother Nature's ten feet tall.

ELUSIVE SLEEP
by Anne Dilley

As I lay in bed and sleep eludes me
I listen to the sounds all around me.

The sounds from outside.

The far off whistle of the train,
The soft hoots of the owls,
The barking of the neighbor's dog,
The nightly chorus of the cats.

All the sounds of loneliness.

I listen to the sounds inside too.

The faint snuffle of our snub-nosed dog,
The hourly announcements of our talking clock,
The whirring sound of the ceiling fan above us,
The quiet and sometimes not so quiet sound of your
snores beside me.

All the sounds that tell me I am not alone.
That I love and am loved.

And safe in those thoughts, sleep no longer eludes me.

THE SMILE

When morning comes and I awake,
A smile is on my face,
Even though the day ahead,
Will be a huge rat race.

The people that I work around,
Think me so very weird,
The way they look at me you'd think,
That food was in my beard.

But smile all day is what I do,
It drives them all insane,
They wonder why I smile so much,
While working in the rain.

A secret that I have from them,
With you I think I'll share,
I smile so much for I have on,
My wife's silk underwear.

MY MUSE

I've wondered long and very hard,
About this thing called muse.
I never knew from whence they came,
These words I write and use.

I always thought they came from me,
To paper from my head,
But now I think that they may come,
From people who are dead.

I see some things within my mind,
These things I try to write.
Sometimes the things I see in there,
Will give me quite a fright.

I feel the ghosts of poets gone,
Have entered into me.
And if I write some pretty verse,
I think I'll let them be.

TOKEN

My heart is pounding in my chest,
As you come near to me,
A vision of my longing dreams,
As you walk by the sea.
The rising sun across the waves,
Puts gold streaks in your hair,
The morning breeze fluffs up your curls,
I see a goddess there.
The sparkling hazel of your eyes,
As you smile sweet at me,
Complements the deep blue-green,
Out on the salty sea.
To see you in this morning light,
A treat beyond compare,
Gives appetite to taste your lips
Here in this salty air.
So gently press your lips to mine,
And let me feel your love.
I'll float among the billowed clouds,
Like angels up above.

SINGING IN THE RYE

I watch the girls as I walk by,
They glean the heather from the rye,
With bottoms up and all heads down,
She seems a mushroom dressed as clown.

A smile upon my weathered face,
Her frown was quick to slow my place,
So lovely is this field of rye,
It puts a twinkle in my eye.

A lively strut gets in my gait,
The thought that one could be my mate,
This field is full of pretty maids,
I stand and watch till daylight fades.

The morning will see my return,
I hope my love she will not spurn,
I'll fiddle and a song I'll sing,
I hope she likes this little ring.

LOVE SONG TO THE SEA

I am awakened
by the sea.
It's calling, calling,
calling me.
I'll go down to
the lapping shore.
Behind me gently
close the door.
I sit down here
in cool wet sand,
And let the ocean
kiss my hand.
A love we have
as none before,
that's why I sit
upon this shore.
I long to live
within the sea,
And with my love
forever be.
The colors in the
ocean deep,
So lovely that
I shall not weep.
The reds and yellows,
blues and greens,
And fish with
multicolored sheens.

The colors of
the setting sun,
Prove now to me
she is the one.
Caressingly
envelope me,
Her liquid arms
hold lovingly.

NOUMENAL PHENOMENON

The object of my full appeal,
Wears not a velvet glove,
A product of my heart and mind,
Phenomenon of love.

Noumental though it seems to be,
A real thing it is not,
But it can bring us lots of joy,
And many tears to blot.

Though what I feel to me is real,
The world with eyes can't see,
It's not a thing to see and touch,
So then how can it be.

Existing in my deepest thoughts,
And in my very soul,
It fills me to the topmost rim,
As if I were a bowl.

It makes me see the good in men,
It masks their evil deeds,
And tells me that a better day
Awaits us with our creeds.

And though my love of all mankind,
Is not a noumenon,
You see what it can make me do,
It's love's phenomenon.

MORNING LIGHT

I'm awoken from my slumber,
By golden streams of light,
The tiny rays are filtered through,
The trees just out of sight.

A zephyr through the sleepy trees,
Makes leaves now slowly sway,
The bluebird's song of happiness
Says it's a brand new day.

The sounds outside, I hear so clear,
The chatter of the squirrel,
I hear the cawing of the crow,
The brook's continued swirl.

Woodpecker tapping on a tree,
The bleating of a sheep,
The sound of chickens as they scratch,
The hood of my old jeep.

A day not unlike many more,
A day for loving life,
A day for saying "I love you"
Unto my darling wife.

GATE SONG

Last night as I slept in my bed,
I had strange dreams inside my head,
I dreamed of dragons in the sky,
And of the time when I must die.

The angels took me to the gate,
They said this was eternal fate,
They said that I must pass the test,
To enter in with all the best.

They said that I must sing a song,
Must make it up and not be wrong,
I must have meter and have rhyme,
Set to a tune in four-four time.

I thought a bit and started slow,
I wasn't sure where it would go,
I sang it low and made it sweet,
Until the tune got to my feet.

Then with a twist I gave a glance,
The angels had begun to dance,
The harps rang out an awesome tune,
The gate flew open right at Noon.

And there inside to my surprise,
A joyous sight for my old eyes,
The poets that I'd known on Earth
Have joined with me in my rebirth.

They joined me in my final song,
We sang and danced the whole night long,
Then it was time to say goodbye,
For I woke up and did not die.

So now I know what will be then,
And I'll be ready once again,
I'll see the ones I love and sing,
It will be such a wondrous thing.

REFLECTIONS
in the Life of a Poet
Chapter Four

VALKYRIES

The day will bring a battle new,
It's outcome is foretold,
The victors of the fight we'll be,
But my blood will run cold.

The Valkyrie has come to me,
She'll take me when I die,
And serve me in the afterlife,
Beneath Valhalla's sky.

My honor it will be to die,
I'm chosen by the queen,
She'll tend to all the needs I have,
Yes, Freyja have I seen.

I now see sunshine in the sky,
The battle will commence,
To Valhalla I will go
To get my recompense.

A hero's death awaits me now,
I'll slay my enemies,
Freyja awaits me as I die
To take me past the seas.

And now as I feel my life's blood,
Spill out upon the ground,
I see the Valkyries arrive,
They're standing all around.

So Freyja, take my offered hand,
And help me to your steed,
And take me to a place of calm,
Where I shall have no need.

STRANGER IN THE HOUSE

A man came by my house today,
He smelled of beer and had a sway,
"I'll make you live forever more,
If you will just unlock the door."

"I'd like a place to rest my head,
Please, do you have an extra bed?
I've been so long upon this path,
I need to rest and have a bath."

I told the man to come on in,
Here is the tub, don't bump your chin,
He was my size, I gave him clothes,
His eyes teared up, he wiped his nose.

I fixed the man a simple meal,
It was good food, but no big deal,
As he was going out the door
He told me what he had come for.

His smell was gone, so was his sway,
He did his job with me today,
"You treated me, a beggar man,
down and out, you lent a hand."

"Forever will your house be blessed,
I am well fed, and now well dressed."
He took two steps and then he veered,
Then turned to air and disappeared.

An angel came to me today,
To see if I would know the way,
The way to treat a stranger here,
Though he may sway and smell of beer.

FINAL PRAYER

One more hour is all I need,
Dear Lord, please hear my plea.
I want to tell my loving wife,
The wonders I shall see.

The stairway up beyond the clouds,
The streets all paved with gold.
To tell her of these wondrous things,
And once more her hand hold.

One hour, Lord, is all I ask,
Then take me up with you.
Where there is only love and peace,
And skies are always blue.

My loving wife is by my side,
I've said my last good-byes.
It's time to go now, take me Lord.
As I now close my eyes.

These were the words I heard that day,
Upon the battlefield.
Five thousand miles he was from home,
When his life he did yield.

His wife he saw, she came to him,
He saw her in his eyes.
Amazing what man's mind can do,
The second that it dies.

WHEN I AM GONE
(a Partenza Represa)

When I am gone and my soul flies,
My soul flies high through Heaven's skies.
Through Heaven's skies it soars so high,
So high that God must soon be nigh.
Be nigh so that my soul can see,
Can see that God has love for me.
For me that is a wondrous thing,
A wondrous thing to my soul bring.
Bring forth and show to all the Earth,
The joy of God in love and mirth.
In love and mirth we see His hand,
His hand will someday rule the land.
The land here where lawless abide,
Lawless abide and do not hide.
And do not hide His love you feel,
His love you feel is a great deal.

REFLECTIONS OF LIFE

Here in the mirror of my mind,
I see my life flow by.
From boy to man a story told,
I try to reason why.

The hard times that have been endured,
The easy times as well.
These thoughts reflect the man I am,
And stories they do tell.

The early times when young of limb,
I had adventures great.
Those are the times I reflect on,
I walked with quickened gait.

These tales I tell with pen and ink,
For all the world to read.
Perhaps for someone young at heart,
These words will plant a seed.

For I can say a happy man,
Is what you see today.
To write my words and have you read,
Sends all my clouds away.

So as I sit and think of times,
Times filled with fun and strife.
I'll write the words that you see now,
Reflections of my life.

MANSION IN THE DARKNESS

As darkness spreads its awesome wings,
And stars the only light,
We sometimes sit and think of things,
That give us such a fright.
The sounds of creatures in the swamp,
The owls hoot through the wood,
I might turn night back into day,
If only that I could.
As on my drink I sit and sip,
On this veranda wide,
The thought I have I will forsake,
To go inside and hide.
You see, I have a purpose here,
I keep a watchful eye,
I watch the darkness all around,
I watch the cloudless sky.
Upon a night much as this one,
He came and took your soul,
To wait for him to come again
Is my eternal goal.
His hooded face I did not see,
But when he comes, I'll know,
And I will not put up a fight,
With him I'll gladly go.
He'll take me to the place you are,
So we can reunite,
No matter if it's dark as pitch,
Our souls will glow with light.

WORK IN PROGRESS

What if I should write a book,
Should I then for a pen name look?
If I should write about an hombre,
Should I use a Spanish nombre?

All these thoughts of little things,
Swirl in my head in tiny rings.
Would bands of gold on lovers hands,
Make me the best in all the lands?

To travel through the stars in verse,
Might seem to some to be quite terse.
To write a book in metered rhyme,
To write about a crack in time.

These things are flapping here inside,
They fill my head where they abide.
The answers that I have are none,
So far I have not even one.

LAUGHTER

The laughter of the children,
A wondrous sound indeed,
The laughter of the women,
With no one left to feed.
These sounds are of the very best,
I've heard in all my life,
And laughter's healing power,
Can forego all our strife.
So let me hear you laugh aloud,
And giggle softly too.
And when I hear these sounds so grand,
I'll laugh along with you.

CROWDED UP THERE

I don't have long to tarry here,
My days are almost done.
I'm going to a better place,
I should have lots off fun.

I'll shake off all the fetters,
That hold me to the ground.
I'll get a set of pearl white wings,
So I can fly around.

I'll look and see the ocean deep,
The mountains up so high,
I'll watch the clouds beneath me,
As they go drifting by.

For in this life I cannot see,
There I'll have eagle's eyes.
And see the world as I soar up,
Up higher than the skies.

But I tell you to mourn me not,
The place that I'm to go.
Will be the best that I could hope,
Not one will e'er feel low.

I'll make a place beside me there,
For crowded it should be.
I'd hate to miss you in the sky,
When Earth shall set you free.

ONE
by Anne Dilley

One

Then another

Friends

Lovers

Unity

Eternal.

WHAT IS A DREAM?
by Anne Dilley

A dream is a vision,
A premonition,
A worthwhile goal.

A dream is something wanted,
Expected,
And longed for.

Dreams are not always practical.
Sometimes what you wind up with
Is not what you wanted.

But look closer.
A dream's possibilities
Are unlimited.

To achieve your dreams, your goal
You must be objective
And set your sights accordingly.

There is no magic to dreaming.
You must work long and hard
To realize your goals.

Don't be discouraged by this.
Have faith, and be persistent
In all you do.

To sum it up then,
A dream...

Is a vision of a possibility.
It is being objective and working hard.
It is being persistent and trying new things.

The fulfillment of a dream
Is a new beginning.

A QUESTION OF QUESTIONS

One day from school I brought a note,
My teacher sent it there.
"Would someone come and talk to me?"
"Someone who might just care."

My Grandpa went to school next day,
To see what might be wrong.
The teacher told him that I asked,
Dumb questions all day long.

"He wants to know details of things,"
"And things he need not know."
My Grandpa simply looked at her,
Emotion did not show.

Then said to her when she was done,
"This is no simple task."
"The only question that is dumb,"
"Is one he doesn't ask."

POET INSIDE

I think that there will always be,
A poet here inside of me.
One who likes to read and write,
With ink of black on parchment white.

The words which cause our hearts to smile,
No malice in the words, no guile.
The love songs in his heart he sings,
To paper he sets many things.

He sings of love and angels wings,
Of cupid's arrows and their stings.
Sometimes on war he will lament,
I think his words are Heaven sent.

He thinks in meter and in rhyme,
He does it at the strangest time.
No matter where I seem to be,
His words he always makes me see.

Some songs to ladies makes them cry,
Some simply ask the question, "why?"
I never know just what he'll say,
I wonder what he'll say today.

Will he be happy or be sad,
And write of good times, or of bad.
This poet my heart longs to see,
Oh, how I wish it could be me.

INDEX

A DIFFERENT MANSION......12

A QUESTION OF QUESTIONS......78

ANGEL ON THE STREET......48-49

BALLAD OF THE TEN GAUGE......36-37

BATTLES......34-35

BEE'S KNEES......16

BREATH OF LIFE......19

CARMELITA......22

CROWDED UP THERE......74

ELUSIVE SLEEP......53

FINAL PRAYER......68

GATE SONG......62-63

GROWN UP......33

HAZARDS OF WRITING......42-43

LAUGHTER......73

LOVE SONG TO THE SEA......58-59

MANSION IN THE DARKNESS......71

MEMORIAL DAY......28

MOONBEAM DREAM......41

MOONLIGHT RENDEZVOUS......24

MORNING LIGHT......61

MOUNTAIN TOP MORNING......52

MY MUSE......55

NATURE'S CHILD......51

NATURE'S SONG......40

NEW BEGINNING......17

NOUMENAL PHENOMENON......60

INDEX

ONE......75

PAINTING IN THE ATTIC......14-15

POET INSIDE......79

REAL MEN DO CRY......29

REFLECTIONS OF LIFE......70

REFLECTIONS......21

RESPECT......32

RUDY REDDINGTON......18

SEA IN LOVE......13

SEA OF LIFE......38-39

SEDUCTRESS...... 50

SHIPWRECKED......20

SILENCE IS LONELY......25

SINGING IN THE RYE......57

SINGING......11

STRANGER IN THE HOUSE......67

THE CHURCHYARD......44-45

THE HAPPY MAN......23

THE SMILE......54

TOKEN......56

TRIBUTE TO THE TEACHERS......31

VALKYRIES......66

WHAT IS A DREAM......76-77

WHEN I AM GONE......69

WORD PAINTING......30

WORK IN PROGRESS......72

www.ingramcontent.com/pod-product-compliance
Lightning Source LLC
Chambersburg PA
CBHW021213020426
42331CB00003B/342